THE CHRISTMAS STORY

Retold & illustrated by

CAROL HEYER

Ideals Children's Books • Nashville, Tennessee

Published by Ideals Publishing Corporation
Nashville, Tennessee 37210

Printed and bound in the United States of America

Library of Congress Cataloging-in-Publication Data

Heyer, Carol, 1950-
The Christmas story / retold & illustrated by Carol Heyer.
    p.   cm.
Summary: Presents the story of Jesus and Christmas and encourages readers to learn the spiritual meaning of holiday gift-giving.
  ISBN 0-8249-8512-5
    1. Jesus Christ—Nativity—Juvenile literature. 2. Christmas—Juvenile literature. [1. Jesus Christ—Nativity. 2. Christmas.]
I. Title.
BT315.2.H44   1991
232.92—dc20   91-9101
                                 CIP
                                 AC

The illustrations in this book are rendered in acrylic paints and using live models.
The text type was set in Garamond #3.
The display type was set in Bauer Text Initials.
Color separations were made by Rayson Films, Inc. of Waukesha, Wisconsin.
Printed and bound by Arcata Graphics Kingsport, Kingsport, Tennessee.

NOW AND ALWAYS, MY WORK IS DEDICATED TO MY PARENTS, WILLIAM AND MERLYN HEYER FOR THEIR UNCEASING SUPPORT AND ENCOURAGEMENT.

MY SPECIAL THANKS TO MODELS DAVID ATKINSON, WILLIAM HEYER, AILSA HUTSON, CARI STERLING, CECILY VOS, AND KATHERINE ZWERS.

- C.H.

At Christmastime we think of wrapping presents and decorating trees. We think of warm cookies and colorful candies. But most of all, we think of Jesus and remember that this time of love and sharing is when we celebrate Jesus' birthday.

Mary, a good and caring young woman, was betrothed to Joseph, a carpenter by trade. When God chose Mary to be the mother of His Son, He sent an angel to her.

The angel Gabriel appeared to Mary and said, "Be happy. God is with you and you have been chosen among women."

But Mary became troubled because she did not understand.

"Do not be afraid, Mary," the angel said, "for you have found favor with God. You will give birth to a Son you will name Jesus. He will be great and will be known as the Son of the Most High."

"How can this be?" asked Mary. "I am not yet married."

The angel answered, "The Holy Spirit will come upon you and you will be with child. The child will be the Son of God."

"May it be as you have said," Mary replied.

As the angel Gabriel departed, the ancient prophecy of the coming of God's Son was soon to be fulfilled.

When Joseph learned of the coming child, he was confused and distressed.

Then one night an angel of the Lord appeared to Joseph in a dream. The angel said to Joseph, "Do not be afraid to take Mary as your wife. The baby she carries is from God. And you must name the child Jesus because he will save the people from their sins."

When Joseph woke up, he knew he must obey the angel, and thus he and Mary began to prepare for the coming child.

Now in those days, Caesar Augustus, the Roman ruler, called for everyone in the Roman Empire to return to the city of their family to be counted. And so it was that Joseph and Mary left Nazareth and set out on the long journey to Bethlehem, the city of Joseph's family.

When Mary and Joseph arrived in Bethlehem, the streets were crowded with others who had also come to register. The inns were filled to overflowing.

As their days in Bethlehem passed, they knew it would soon be time for the baby's birth. They searched for a place to stay, but there was no room for them anywhere.

Weary and heavy with child, Mary trusted that Joseph would find a place for her to have her baby.

Finally, near the edge of town, they found a stable for shelter. There, along with the animals and their babies, Mary and Joseph were at last able to rest.

In the soft hay and dim light of the stable, Mary delivered her firstborn child, the Son of God. Mary wrapped the child in large, soft cloths and laid him in a straw-filled manger. They named him Jesus, as the angel had instructed many months before.

For hundreds of years, the prophets had spoken of the coming of the Savior whose kingdom would never end. And on that quiet night in Bethlehem, the prophecies were fulfilled in a tiny baby boy who lay sleeping in a manger.

In the nearby fields, the shepherds who protected their sheep throughout the night suddenly saw an angel of the Lord before them. The glory of the Lord shone down around them, and they were terrified.

"Do not be afraid," the angel said, "because I bring you happy news. This day in Bethlehem is born to you a Savior. He is Christ the Lord.

"You will find him wrapped in swaddling cloths and lying in a manger."

And suddenly, all around the angel appeared many more angels who began praising God and singing "Glory to God in the highest, and on earth peace among men of goodwill!"

As soon as the angels left them, the shepherds said to one another, "Let us go to Bethlehem and see this thing that has happened, which the Lord has told us about."

They hurried to see the baby Jesus, and found him lying in the manger just as the angel had said.

The shepherds spread far and wide the story of the angel's message, and of the birth of Christ. And the people who heard the stories were filled with wonder and curiosity.

When Jesus was born, a brilliant star appeared in the sky. Far away in the east lived wise men who studied both the skies and the prophecies. When the star appeared, they knew that it marked the birth of a great king, the king of the Jews. They noted the time and day of the star's appearance and then set out at once to find their king.

During the many months that the wise men journeyed, the time came for the baby Jesus to be presented at the temple. Forty days after his birth, as custom dictated, Mary and Joseph took Jesus to the temple to present him to God.

They were met in the temple by Simeon, a devout and holy man. When Simeon saw the baby, he knew that Jesus was the Messiah, the fulfillment of the prophecy, and he was overjoyed.

The prophet Anna was also in the temple. Anna lived there day and night, fasting, praying, and waiting for the Messiah to come. She too recognized the baby as the Son of God and she gave praise to the Lord. From that moment on, she told all that she met that Jesus was the Savior of the world.

As the wise men continued on their long journey to find the king, they came to Jerusalem, where they stopped to ask King Herod where they could find the young king. Herod called together his chief priests and teachers of the law and asked them where Christ was to be born.

"In Bethlehem of Judea," they told him. Explaining the ancient prophecy, the priests reminded Herod that long ago it was written:

> *But you Bethlehem, in the land of Judea, are by no means least*
> *among the rulers of Judea; for out of you will come a ruler who*
> *will be the shepherd of my people Israel.*

Herod and his followers were frightened. Who was this baby who could grow up to be king and take away their leadership?

"Go and make a careful search for the child," Herod said to the wise men. "As soon as you find him, report to me so that I, too, may go and worship the king," he lied.

The three wise men gathered their servants and their belongings and continued on their journey, heading to Bethlehem and to the little king.

As they traveled, the star lighted their way and led them on until it finally stopped over the place where the baby Jesus lay.

Overjoyed to find the child with Mary and Joseph, the wise men knelt down and worshiped him. They gave the baby their treasures: gold because he was king; frankincense because he was God; and myrrh because he was man.

Later, when the wise men slept, they were warned in a dream not to tell King Herod or his followers where to find Jesus because Herod wanted to hurt the baby. When the time came for the wise men to leave, they took a different route home, one that allowed them to avoid Jerusalem and Herod altogether.

King Herod remained angered by the birth of the Messiah. When the wise men did not report to him, he made plans to have the child killed. But one night as Joseph slept, an angel warned him of the danger.

"Take the baby and his mother far away into Egypt," the angel said. "And stay there until I tell you that it is safe to return."

So little Jesus spent the first few years of his life in the hot Egyptian sun. Finally, King Herod died, and the angel appeared to Joseph, telling him that they could at last leave Egypt in safety.

The family returned to Nazareth, where Jesus grew to be a strong young boy. He especially loved to learn from his teachers in the temple, listening carefully and asking questions.

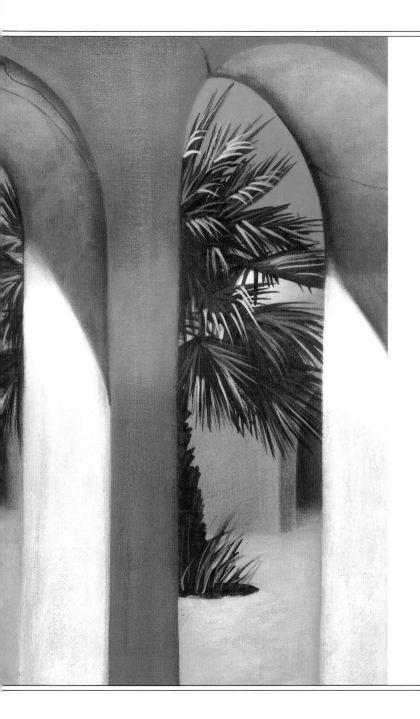

Jesus began his ministry when he was about thirty years old, teaching the truth and the gospel of love. Followers gathered around him wherever he went, and he soon had twelve strong disciples who followed his teaching and spread his word to others.

When the time for Jesus' death came to pass, he had already left on earth his many lessons on how to serve God and how to have eternal life. He had performed many miracles and healed many people, and finally, through his death and Resurrection, he saved us all.

This is why Christians celebrate Christmas. We remember that Jesus was born to save us and to give us hope. On Christmas morning, we remember the wise men's gifts by giving and receiving presents of our own. And we go to church to honor Jesus and to thank God for sending us His Son to give us the gift of everlasting life.